CREATIVE EDUCATION

NFL TODAY

ARIZONA CARDINALS

JOHN NICHOLS

Published by Creative Education
123 South Broad Street, Mankato, Minnesota 56001
Creative Education is an imprint of The Creative Company

Designed by Rita Marshall

Photos by: Allsport USA, AP/Wide World Photos, Bettmann/CORBIS,
SportsChrome

Library of Congress Cataloging-in-Publication Data

Nichols, John, 1966–
Arizona Cardinals / by John Nichols.
p. cm. — (NFL today)
Summary: Traces the history of the team from its beginnings through 1999.
ISBN 1-58341-034-1

1. Arizona Cardinals (Football team)—History—Juvenile literature. [1. Arizona
Cardinals (Football team)—History. 2. Football—History.] I. Title. II. Series:
NFL today (Mankato, Minn.)

GV956.A75N53   2000
796.332'64'0979173—dc21   99-015761

First edition

9 8 7 6 5 4 3 2 1

One of the first settlers along Arizona's Salt River was an Englishman named Darrel Dupa. Noticing that the settlers were building a new town atop the ruins of an old Native American community, he was reminded of the legend of the phoenix, a mythical bird that burned up but was then reborn from its own ashes. He soon named the town Phoenix.

Over time, Phoenix grew from a small town to a booming city. The area's sunny climate, clean air, and beautiful desert scenery has lured tens of thousands of new residents—and one professional football team. In 1988, the St. Louis Cardinals franchise of the National Football League relocated in

One of football's first great halfbacks, Ernie Nevers.

the Phoenix area, seeking to attract a new group of fans and to achieve a rebirth of its old glory in the league.

The Arizona Cardinals have one of the newer names in the NFL, but the team isn't new. In fact, it is the oldest professional football franchise in the United States, born long before the NFL was established. The team began playing in Chicago back in 1899, then found its way to St. Louis in 1960 before heading out west in 1988.

Halfback John "Paddy" Driscoll set a franchise record by scoring 27 points in a single game.

Although the club has won only two league championships over the years and has missed the playoffs most seasons, many Cardinals stars have earned high places in NFL history. The Pro Football Hall of Fame has welcomed numerous former Cardinals greats, including Ernie Nevers, Paddy Driscoll, Ollie Matson, Larry Wilson, and Jackie Smith. Cardinals fans from Chicago to Arizona also have a special place in their hearts for such former stars as quarterbacks Jim Hart and Neil Lomax; running backs Ottis Anderson and Terry Metcalf; and receivers Roy Green and Mel Gray.

In recent years, Arizona fans have cheered for a new generation of football heroes led by young quarterback Jake Plummer. With Plummer and other talented young players on the rise, Cardinals fans appear to be in for a rebirth of thrilling football in the Arizona desert.

A NORMAL START

The Arizona Cardinals franchise not only began its existence in a different city, but it started with a different name, too. In 1899, a Chicago painter and builder named Chris O'Brien gathered several friends and family members

Andre Wadsworth dominated with both power and quickness.

Star guard Walt Kiesling helped the Cardinals jump to a 6–6–1 record.

together to form the Morgan Athletic Club. O'Brien later moved the club's home to Chicago's Normal Field, and everyone began calling the team the "Normals." When O'Brien made a deal for some bright-red secondhand jerseys from the University of Chicago, he gave the team a new name, the "Cardinals," to fit its new uniforms.

When the NFL was formed in the early 1920s, the Cardinals immediately became one of the league's top teams, thanks mainly to star player John "Paddy" Driscoll. An outstanding halfback on offense and cornerback on defense, Driscoll also drop-kicked field goals and tripled as the team's head coach. Driscoll led the club to an 11–2–1 record and its first NFL championship in 1925.

Unfortunately, the city of Chicago was in love with another local football team—the Bears. Attendance for Cardinals games remained low, and the club's financial picture became bleak. O'Brien was forced to sell Driscoll to the Bears following the championship season, and then, after three straight losing seasons, he sold the entire franchise to a Chicago doctor named David Jones.

NEVERS NEVER QUITS

The Cardinals' new owner had a plan to make the team a winner again. The man at the center of that plan was Ernie Nevers, who had gained national fame as a bruising halfback at Stanford University. In 1929, Jones convinced the 6-foot-1 and 210-pound Nevers to sign with the Cardinals as a player-coach. Finally, the Cardinals had a star exciting enough to steal the headlines from the Bears.

"People used to say I should try to avoid getting hit," Nevers recalled years later. "But that wasn't football to me. What it was all about was making a tackler know you were around. That's what football was meant for—contact. I guess I got the greatest satisfaction out of popping a lineman—you know, really laying into him—and then going on to somebody else."

In his first season with the Cardinals, Nevers got a chance to show just how good he was, and, best of all, he did it against the Bears. "I don't need to tell you about Nevers," Bears head coach George Halas told his players before the game between the Chicago rivals. "If you stop him, you stop the Cardinals." That was easier said than done.

As sportswriter Phil Berger described, "Everybody in Comiskey Park the afternoon of November 28 knew what would happen. Very simply, Ernie Nevers would try to destroy the Bears by himself." He tried, and he did. The 8,000 fans in attendance watched in disbelief as Nevers dismantled the Bears' defense, scoring six touchdowns and four extra points in a 40–6 Cardinals romp. Nevers's remarkable one-game scoring performance has never been matched by any other NFL player.

Nevers was a winner, but the Cardinals weren't. He played for and coached the Cardinals through the 1931 season and then retired. A year later, David Jones decided to sell the team to Chicago businessman Charles W. Bidwill Sr. for $50,000. Still, a new owner didn't change the club's luck. From 1933 to 1946, the Cardinals never rose above fourth place in the Western Division, losing approximately three out of every four games they played.

1 9 3 1

Ernie Nevers retired with 26 career rushing touchdowns—a new Cardinals record.

Explosive rusher Ottis Anderson.

Roy Green starred as a cornerback, receiver, and kick returner. 11

1 9 4 8

Fleet-footed half-back Charley Trippi led the team with 690 rushing yards.

In 1946, Bidwill made a move that would turn the team around. He rehired Jimmy Conzelman as coach. Conzelman had led the Cardinals through losing campaigns from 1940 to 1942. This time, though, Bidwill would give him plenty of talent with which to work.

"I've got a dream," Conzelman told reporters. "You have to have horses in the backfield, otherwise you're a doormat. I want the greatest backfield in the league—the best passer and the best runners. When I have all of that going for me, I'll have the professional championship in my pocket."

Conzelman explained his plan to the team owner and guaranteed an NFL title if the right personnel were brought in. Bidwill agreed to spend the money needed to acquire Conzelman's "Dream Backfield," and the coach began his search. Conzelman brought together quarterback Paul Christman, halfbacks Elmer Angsman Jr. and Marshall Goldberg, and fullback Pat Harder in 1946. He completed the backfield a year later by drafting lightning-quick halfback Charley Trippi from the University of Georgia and signing him to the richest contract in league history—$100,000 for four years.

The "Dream Backfield" led the Cardinals to a 9–3 record in 1947, good enough for the Western Division title ahead of the second-place Bears. In the 1947 NFL championship game, the Cardinals outscored the Philadelphia Eagles 28–21. Conzelman had kept his promise, but owner Charles Bidwill wasn't around to see it. He had died during the 1947 season. The following year, the Cardinals won another division title with an 11–1 record—the best in team history—and again met the Eagles for the NFL title. This time, however, Philadelphia came out on top, 7–0.

Conzelman decided to step down after the 1948 season, and the Cards went into a tailspin. They slumped to third place in 1949 and then posted six straight losing seasons after the club was shifted to the NFL's Eastern Division. The one bright spot for Cardinals fans during those years was the play of running back Ollie Matson, a future Pro Football Hall-of-Famer.

Matson joined the Cardinals in 1952 after winning two track medals in the 1952 Summer Olympics in Helsinki, Finland. He quickly established himself as a triple-threat star—rushing, receiving, and returning kicks. Unfortunately, Matson couldn't turn the team around by himself. Before the 1959 season, the Cards traded Matson to the Los Angeles Rams and got nine players in return—though he was probably better than all nine put together.

The Cardinals were willing to give up Matson because they had two young halfbacks ready to take over the team's rushing and pass-receiving duties. John David Crow, a former Heisman Trophy winner, was an outstanding runner, and Bobby Joe Conrad was an excellent pass catcher.

The two players got their chance to star, but not in Chicago. Before the 1960 season, the Bidwill family decided that the Cardinals were no longer going to play second-fiddle to the more popular Bears. After 60 years in Chicago, the team moved to St. Louis, Missouri.

The change of scenery improved the team's fortunes. Led by Crow, Conrad, wide receiver Sonny Randle, and a fine

1 9 5 6

Ollie Matson carried the ball 192 times for 924 yards—both new club records.

13

1 9 6 0

Receiver Sonny Randle represented the Cardinals in the first Pro Bowl.

young quarterback named Charley Johnson, the Cardinals began to move up in the NFL's Eastern Division. Crow soon won over the St. Louis fans by gaining 1,071 yards in his first season in Missouri, while Randle caught a league-leading 15 touchdown passes. Their heroics helped the Cardinals record their second winning season (6–5–1) in a decade.

By 1963, new coach Wally Lemm could also call on the offensive skills of fullback Bill "Thunder" Thornton and flanker Bob Paremore, a world-class sprinter. He also added place-kicker Jim Bakken, who would have a remarkable 17-year career in St. Louis, setting franchise records for consecutive games played and points scored. This gathering of talent, under Charley Johnson's on-field leadership, helped the Cardinals jump to 9–5 in 1963 and 9–3–2 in 1964.

For the next few years, the Cards had both good and bad seasons, but better days were ahead for St. Louis fans. Slowly but surely, the Cardinals acquired the players who would make up one of the most exciting and dangerous offensive teams in the NFL during the 1970s.

HART AND GRAY MAKE "AIR CORYELL" FLY

The Cardinals' first new offensive star arrived in St. Louis in 1966. Jim Hart was a little-known quarterback from a little-known nearby college called Southern Illinois-Carbondale. Hart wasn't even drafted by an NFL team. The Cardinals acquired him as a free agent, and though he wasn't expected to stick around long, Hart would end up playing 18 seasons in St. Louis and setting most of the team's passing records before he retired.

Star defensive back Tim McDonald.

Offensive lineman Dan Dierdorf.

Hart's leadership made a definite improvement in the St. Louis offense, but he needed more help. That assistance began arriving through the 1971 NFL draft, when the Cardinals picked up Missouri wide receiver Mel Gray, noted more for his track and field talent than his football skills. Many experts considered Gray to be just a sprinter who wouldn't be able to hold on to the ball when he was hit by tacklers.

"They said I couldn't catch the ball—that my hands were like bricks," Gray recalled. Despite such criticism, Gray quickly became one of the most dangerous deep threats in the league. He averaged nearly 30 yards a catch in his rookie year and caught four long touchdown passes. "Gray proved conclusively that speed and agility will beat weight and height anytime," wrote *Sports Illustrated* reporter Rick Telander.

Hart and Gray were joined in 1973 by halfback Terry Metcalf, an exceptional receiver, runner, and kick returner. But the key to the offense may have actually been the All-Pro linemen doing the blocking: center Tom Banks, tackle Dan Dierdorf, and guard Conrad Dobler. They gave Hart time to pass and Metcalf room to run. They also made it possible for new Cardinals coach Don Coryell to install a passing offense that became known around the league as "Air Coryell."

Air Coryell revved up in 1973 and was in full gear by 1974. That year, St. Louis won its first seven games of the season, including a thrilling 31–28 win over the defending Eastern Division champion Dallas Cowboys. The key play in that game was an 80-yard touchdown strike to Mel Gray. "They were trying to play me one-on-one, and that made me smile," Gray said. "I guess maybe people will start taking us seriously now."

1 9 7 0

Star tight end Jackie Smith was named to his fifth straight Pro Bowl.

*All-Pro guard
Conrad Dobler
anchored a stout
offensive line for
the fourth season.*

The three-point win over Dallas was typical of the 1974 season for the Cardinals. Every game that year was close—sometimes a little too close for St. Louis fans, who started calling their team the "Cardiac Cardinals" because of all the heart-stopping finishes. "I guess if there's a way to make a game closer, we'll think of it," said Coryell.

Despite a late-season fade, the Cardinals finished 10–4 and won their first division title since 1947. Unfortunately, the team's long-awaited return to the playoffs was short-lived. The Minnesota Vikings sent them home early with a 30–14 loss in the first round.

St. Louis won another Eastern Division title in 1975 with an 11–3 record. Terry Metcalf had a remarkable year, gaining an NFL-record 2,462 yards rushing, receiving, and returning kickoffs and punts. Running back Jim Otis also asserted himself that year, gaining 1,076 rushing yards to balance the Cardinals' air attack. But in the playoffs, St. Louis couldn't stop the running game of the Los Angeles Rams, losing 35–23 in the first round. Coryell's Cardiac Cardinals kept winning close ones in 1976, finishing 10–4, but two tough losses to the Washington Redskins cost the team a playoff berth.

The team's fortunes declined after that. Coryell was fired following a 7–7 year in 1977. Metcalf left the team in 1978 after a contract dispute. Even Mel Gray seemed to be slowing down. However, in the 1979 draft, the Cardinals found another speedster named Roy Green who would eventually take Gray's place as the team's deep threat. St. Louis also added an outstanding runner named Ottis Anderson.

Roy Green came out of tiny Henderson State University in Arkansas—not exactly a hotbed of pro football talent. But

Green proved to be something special. He was drafted as a cornerback and started his pro career on defense. He also returned kickoffs and tied an NFL record with a 106-yard return against Dallas in his rookie year.

But during the 1981 season, Cardinals coach Jim Hanifan asked Green to take on additional offensive duties as a wide receiver. "I just want you to go in and run by everybody," Hanifan told him. Green didn't know much about the Cardinals' offense, but he didn't really have to. He was a secret weapon whose job was to go deep as fast as he could. "It didn't matter what they called in the huddle," Green laughed. "I knew what I was doing."

When Green caught a 60-yard bomb from Jim Hart in his first game on offense, the St. Louis secret was out. He con-

1 9 7 7

Don Coryell left St. Louis after compiling a 42–29–1 coaching record.

Terry Metcalf captivated fans with his speed and slick moves.

Jim Hart piloted the Cardinals' "Air Coryell" offense.

tinued to play both offense and defense throughout the 1981 season and earned the nickname "Jet Stream" Green for his blinding speed. Green caught and intercepted passes in three different games, something that had not been done by any NFL player since 1957. "The only thing that Roy hasn't done is tape our ankles," joked Dan Dierdorf. "Maybe a lot of guys could play both ways, but it's one thing to say you're able to and another to actually do it. In a game of gifted athletes, Roy is exceptional."

While Green was the team's new star through the airways, Ottis Anderson was grinding out yardage on the ground and setting one team record after another. In 1979, the rookie runner from Miami bulled over defenders for 1,605 yards—still a franchise one-year rushing record.

1 9 8 0

Pro-Bowler Roger Wehrli anchored the Cardinals' secondary for the 12th season.

LOMAX BRINGS OFFENSE TO MAXIMUM EFFICIENCY

Roy Green and Ottis Anderson were not the only new faces on offense in St. Louis in the early 1980s. After a series of lopsided losses during the 1981 season, Coach Hanifan decided to bench Jim Hart in favor of rookie quarterback Neil Lomax. The young passer had set several records at Portland State University, where he played both football and baseball. Doubling as a quarterback and a pitcher, Lomax was confident he could do a good job both on the field and on the mound. "I have always felt that I can complete a pass or strike out a batter," Lomax explained. "I have always wanted to be the . . . take-charge kind of guy. Every play, I go all out to execute the best that I can. That's what good players do."

Neil Lomax completed 37 passes for 468 yards in a single game—both new team records.

In his first four games as a pro starter, Lomax led the Cardinals to four straight victories. Suddenly, the once-hopeless Cards were in contention for a playoff spot. The team lost its last two games, however, to finish at 7–9. The club did make the playoffs in the strike-shortened 1982 season but suffered a first-round loss to the Green Bay Packers.

By 1983, Lomax and Green had become the best quarterback-receiver combination in the league, combining for 78 passes, 1,227 yards, and a league-leading 14 touchdowns. Their explosiveness, combined with Ottis Anderson's power, helped the Cardinals record winning seasons in both 1983 and 1984. The team failed to qualify for the playoffs each year, but they came very close in 1984.

Going into that year's final game, St. Louis needed to beat the Washington Redskins to earn a postseason berth. The Redskins burst out to a 23–7 halftime lead, and things looked pretty bleak for St. Louis. Then Lomax took charge in the second half, hitting Green for two touchdowns and setting up two Neil O'Donoghue field goals that brought the Cards within two points. With four seconds to go, O'Donoghue attempted a 50-yard field goal for the win. This time his kick fell inches short of the goal posts, and the Cardinals' season was over.

A year later, the Cardinals began to fall in the standings. The biggest problem was injuries, as Lomax, Green, and Anderson spent numerous games on the sidelines. During losing seasons in 1985, 1986, and 1987, St. Louis fans began to lose interest in the Cardinals. As fan attendance dropped, team owner William Bidwill contemplated relocating the franchise once again.

In March 1988, Bidwill received permission from the league to take his team to Phoenix, and the club headed west. Playing in Sun Devil Stadium in nearby Tempe, the Cards got off to a great start in 1988, going 7–4 and seeming destined for a playoff berth. Neil Lomax, finally back from injuries, was having his best season ever, amassing more than 3,400 yards passing in the first 11 games. J.T. Smith and Roy Green were each nearing 1,000 receiving yards, and running backs Earl Ferrell and Stump Mitchell were both having strong seasons as well. Then Lomax began having injury problems again, however, and the club fell apart, losing its last five games to finish a disappointing 7–9.

Pro-Bowl receiver J.T. Smith burned the Redskins for four touchdowns in one game.

Lomax retired after the 1988 season, and Arizona fell into a tailspin, posting losing records the next five seasons. Finally, in 1994, Bidwell tried to shake the franchise from its losing ways by hiring Buddy Ryan as head coach and general manager. Ryan had played a part in building powerhouse teams in Chicago, Philadelphia, and Houston, but he was just as well-known for his confrontational personality.

Unfortunately, Ryan's weaknesses as a coach were revealed during his two-year stay in Arizona. Ryan built a hard-hitting defense led by massive tackle Eric Swann and swift cornerback Aeneas Williams, but the offense lacked direction. "Buddy loved defense, and he loved figuring out ways to stop other teams," noted new Cardinals quarterback Dave Krieg. "But he didn't seem to care much about what we did offensively. It was almost like offense was an afterthought for him." After the Cardinals lost seven of their final eight games in 1995—including a 27–7 drubbing at the hands of the expansion Carolina Panthers—Ryan was fired.

Dangerous quarterback Jake "the Snake" Plummer (pages 26-27).

Halfback Larry Centers caught 101 passes, setting a new NFL record for running backs.

After the firing of Ryan, the Cardinals brought in former Indianapolis defensive coordinator Vince Tobin to lead the team in a new direction. Tobin welcomed the challenge of turning around the Cardinals. "People tell me that we can't build a winner here in Arizona," Tobin told reporters. "I've heard all the excuses—it's too hot, Phoenix isn't a football town. All that's a bunch of baloney. We can do it and it all starts today."

The Cardinals took a big step toward realizing their new coach's goal by producing a 7–9 record in 1996. Rookie defensive lineman Simeon Rice burst upon the scene with 12.5 quarterback sacks, tying the NFL rookie record. "I think we are on to something here," said Pro-Bowl cornerback Aeneas Williams. "We've got some of the pieces here, but we need more."

One of the pieces the Cardinals needed was a quarterback. Veterans Dave Krieg and Boomer Esiason had given the Cardinals some good performances, but both were past their prime. In the 1997 NFL draft, the Cardinals acquired Arizona State University quarterback Jake Plummer with their second-round pick.

Plummer had already captured the hearts of Arizona football fans by leading the Sun Devils to an undefeated regular season in 1996 and a trip to the Rose Bowl. The young quarterback had an exciting, scrambling style that allowed him to strike for big plays from any place on the field. In fact, he had become so renowned for his slick playmaking that Arizona State fans had nicknamed him Jake "the Snake."

Although Plummer excelled in college, many pro teams thought that the 6-foot-2 and 190-pound quarterback was too frail and lacked the cannon arm needed to play in the NFL. Coach Tobin had no such doubts. "I look at whether the kid can make a difference on the football field," explained the Cardinals' head man. "Jake is as skinny as a rail, but he is a whale of a football player."

Although the Cardinals posted a 4–12 record in 1997, their young quarterback got a little better each week. By the end of the season, Plummer had thrown for 2,203 yards and 15 touchdowns. Late in the season, he also set an NFL rookie record by shredding the New York Giants for 388 yards passing.

In 1998, Plummer picked up the Cardinals franchise—which had gone more than 50 years without a postseason victory—and carried it farther than any fan could have imagined. The Cardinals opened the season by getting hammered in their first two games, but Plummer then led Arizona to a 9–7 finish—good enough to qualify for the playoffs as a Wild Card team.

In the Cardinals' first playoff game in 16 years, they faced their division rival, the Dallas Cowboys. Although Dallas had beaten Arizona twice during the regular season, the Cardinals demolished the Cowboys 20–7. Although Arizona fell to the Minnesota Vikings the next week, the young Cardinals had won over grateful Arizona fans.

With the playoff win fresh in their minds, hopes for a banner 1999 season ran high among the Cardinals faithful. Unfortunately, the young talent that shone so brightly in 1998 took a step backward in 1999.

1 9 9 9

End Simeon Rice stormed through opposing lines for a team-record 16 quarterback sacks.

Acrobatic wide receiver Rob Moore.

One of the league's finest man-to-man defenders, Aeneas Williams. 31

Linebacker Ronald McKinnon was one of Arizona's most feared tacklers.

Eric Swann and end Andre Wadsworth missed several games with injuries, crippling the Cardinals' usually fearsome defense. Plummer also suffered numerous injuries, including a broken finger on his throwing hand, that sent him to the bench for four weeks. Although he showed his toughness by returning to the lineup, his still-healing hand limited his effectiveness.

With their star quarterback hobbled and their defense missing two key players, the Cardinals fell to a disappointing 6–10. "It was a hard lesson to learn," Plummer said after the season. "This game will humble you in a hurry. We got knocked down. Now it's up to all of us to get back up and rededicate ourselves to winning."

The Cardinals will count on Plummer to shine like a star in Arizona's desert sky for a long time. With "The Snake" leading such young stars as running back Thomas Jones—the team's top pick in the 2000 draft—fans hope that the club that originated in the Midwest and was reborn in Phoenix will soon rise from the ashes to capture a Super Bowl championship.